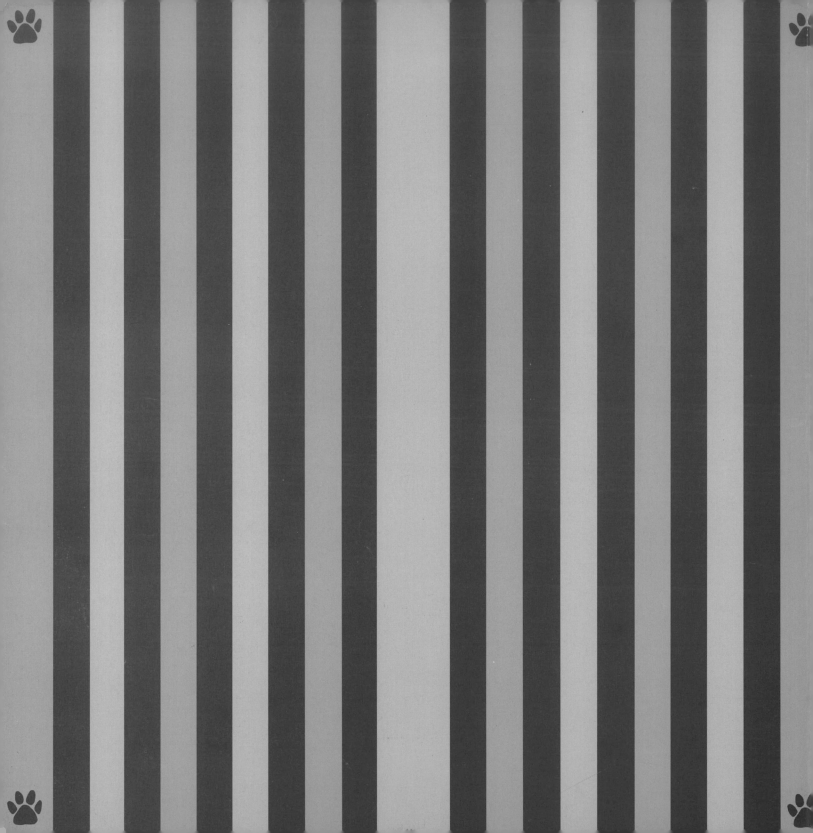

Vet

Written by Sue Barraclough
Photography by Chris Fairclough

W

FRANKLIN WATTS
LONDON • SYDNEY

This edition 2010
First published in 2006 by Franklin Watts
338 Euston Road, London NW1 3BH

Franklin Watts Australia
Level 17/207 Kent Street
Sydney NSW 2000

Editor: Adrian Cole
Designer: Jemima Lumley
Art direction: Jonathan Hair
Photography: Chris Fairclough

**This book is dedicated to the memory of Buttons,
a fun-loving cat who lived life to the full.**

Thanks to Su, Nigel and all the staff at the Blue Cross Animal Hospital,
Victoria, London, and to Sue, Christine, Amy and David for all their help.

A CIP catalogue record for this book is available
from the British Library

ISBN 978 0 7496 9663 4

Dewey decimal classification number: 636.089

Printed in China

Franklin Watts is a division of Hachette Children's Books,
an Hachette UK company.
www.hachette.co.uk

Contents

I am a vet

My name is Nigel. I am a vet, which means that I treat sick animals. I work in an animal hospital.

I work with a team
of vets and other staff.
Nurses help look after
the animals, too.

A nurse often helps
when I am examining
an animal.

Starting work

When I arrive at the hospital, people are already waiting with their pets. I change into my white coat so I can start work.

First, I look at an x-ray of a cat with a broken leg. It came to the hospital last night. I may have to treat this cat later.

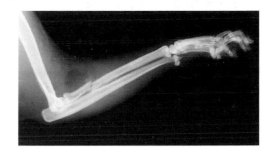

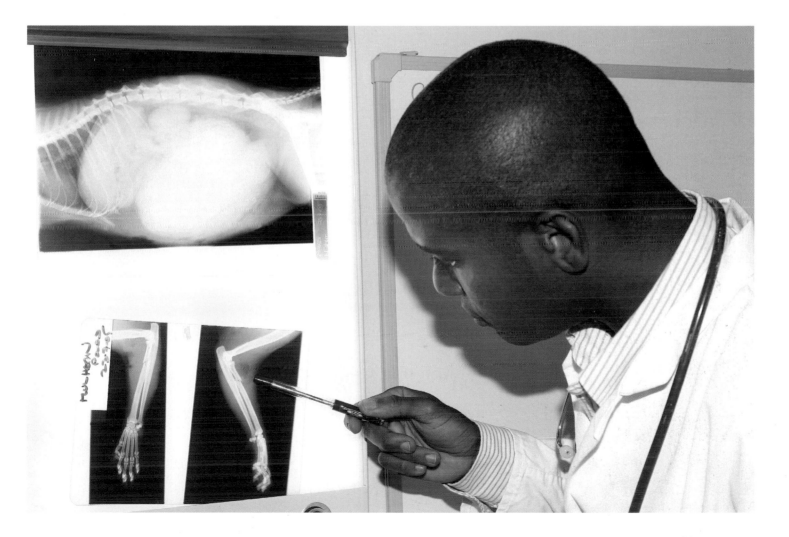

Working in the clinic

I work part of my day in the clinic, where animals are brought in. I check the computer to find out what animal is booked in first. Then I find out if I have treated it before.

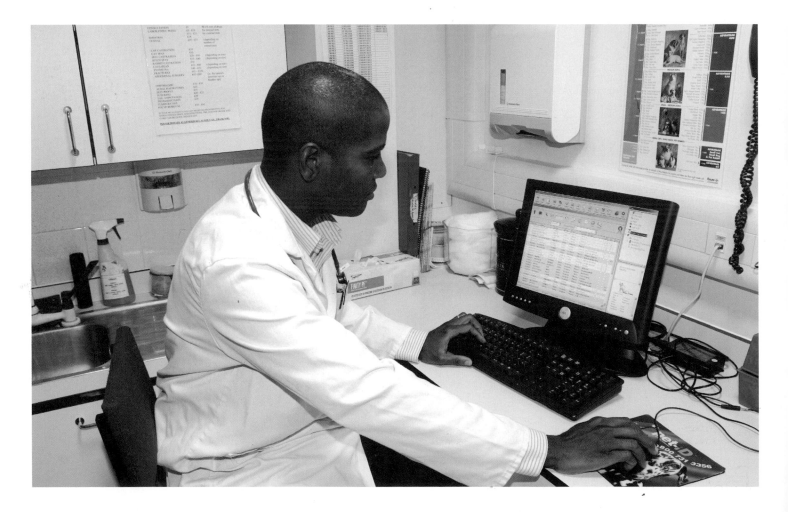

In the waiting room, people
wait with their pets. David
has brought in his cat,
Buttons, who is unwell.

Calling in a patient

I call David and his family into the examination room. They bring Buttons in with them.

David tells me that Buttons has been sick and has not been eating his food.

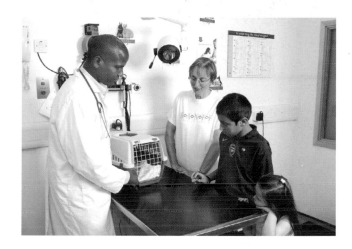

We get Buttons out of the box carefully. All animals are scared when they come to see a vet. I make sure Buttons cannot run away.

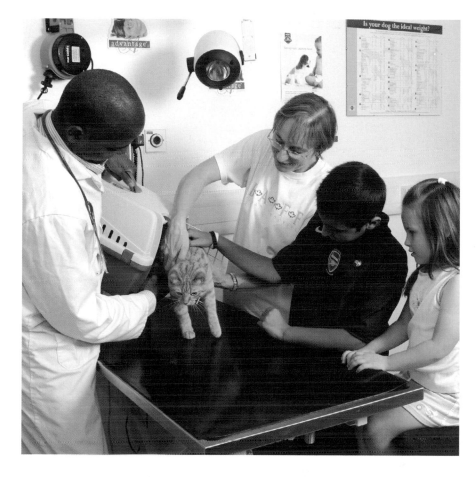

Doing health checks

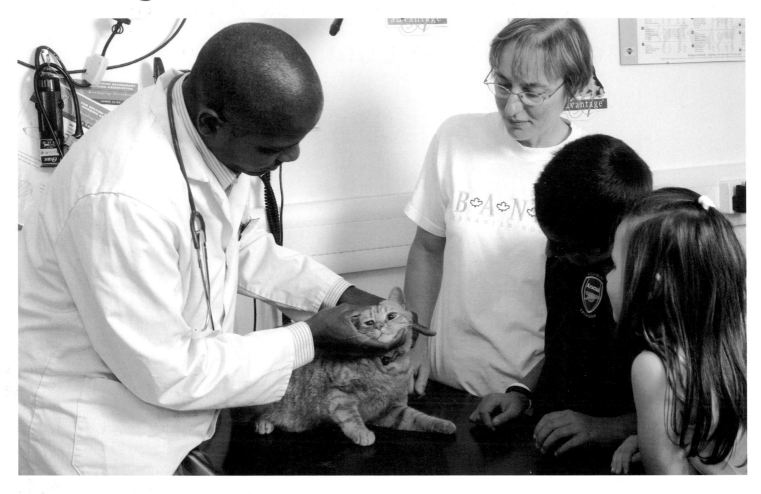

I check Buttons' eyes, teeth and ears. I also look for any obvious problems.

I weigh Buttons. I want to check if he has lost weight since the last time I saw him.

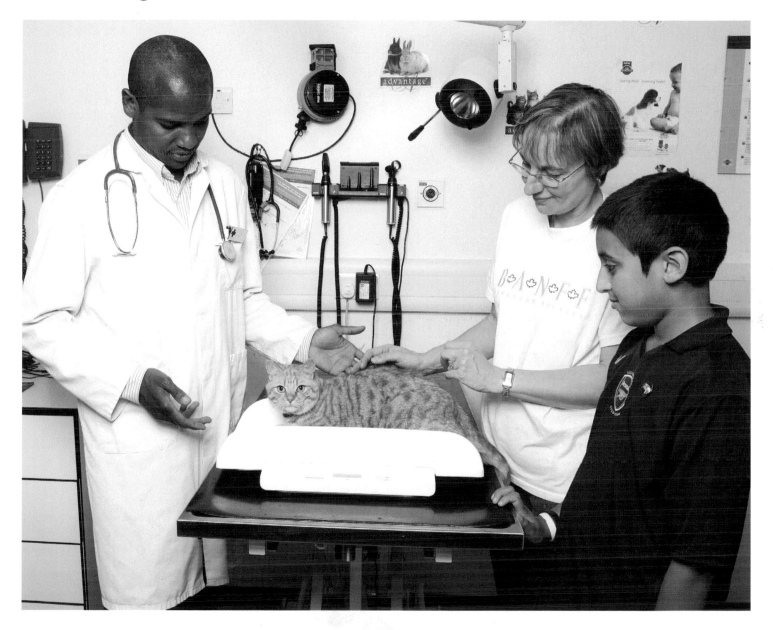

Deciding on treatment

Buttons has a problem with his teeth. He will need some medicine to get better. I help David to put Buttons carefully into his box.

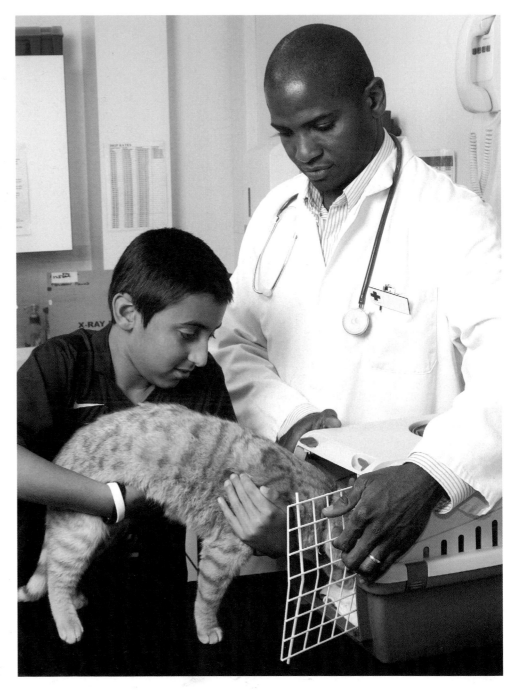

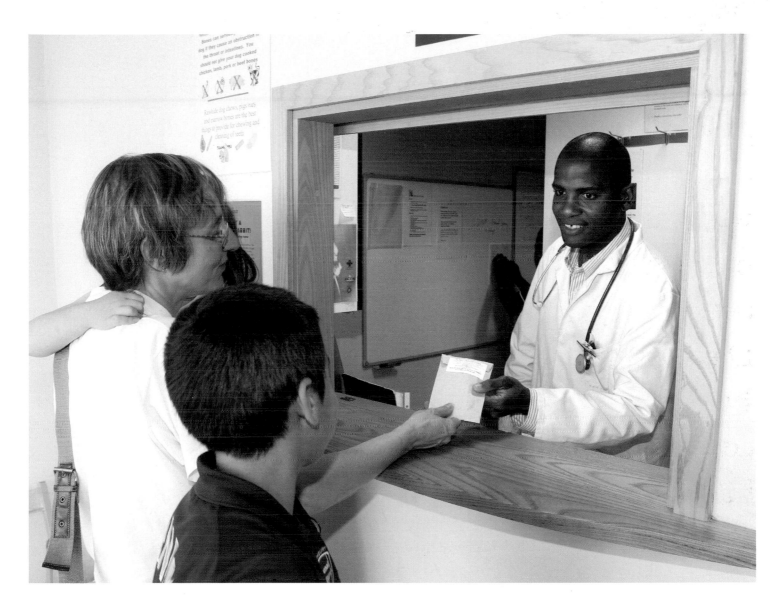

Before David goes home I make sure
he and his mum pick up the medicine for
Buttons. Then I get ready for my next patient.

Getting ready to operate

After the clinic I help to train student vets who are working at the hospital. We talk about the animals that need operations.

I put on special gear to work in the operating theatre. Everything I wear is sterilised.

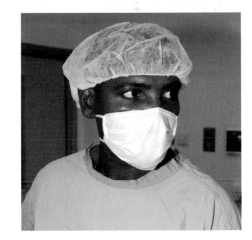

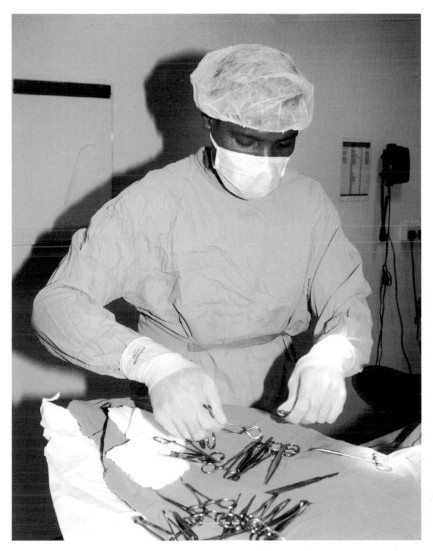

The operating theatre is very clean. All the instruments are specially cleaned too. A clean set is used for each operation.

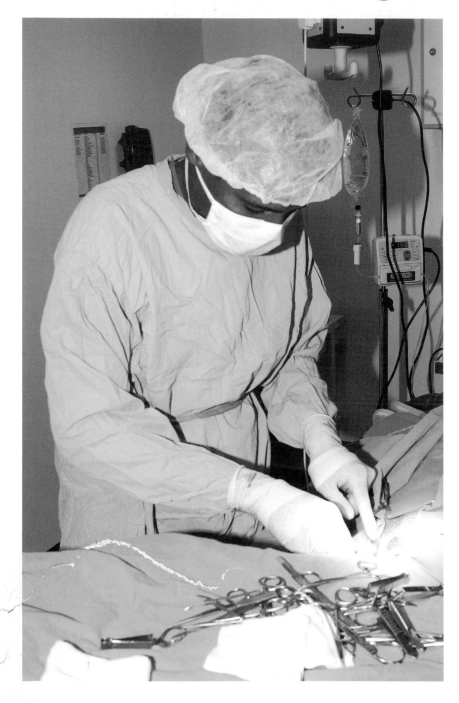

This dog has been given drugs to make sure it won't feel any pain. I cover the whole dog with a green cloth, except for the area I want to work on.

When I have finished the operation, I sew up the wound and clean it. The dog is taken to the recovery area.

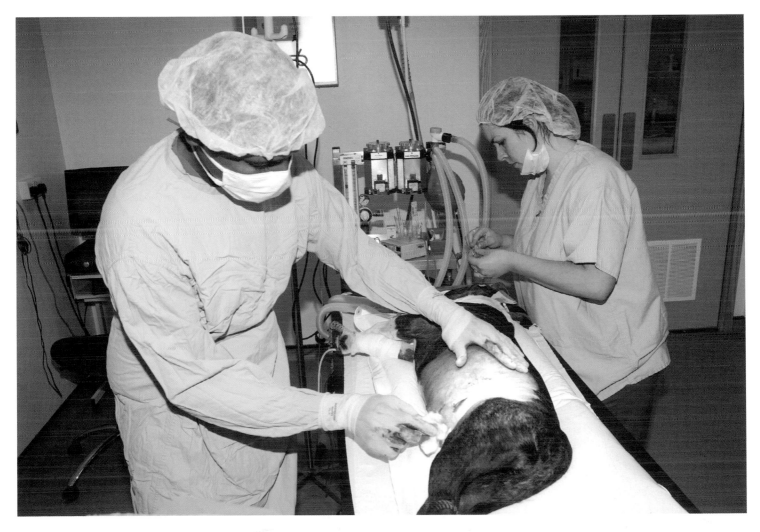

Visiting the recovery area

The recovery area is where animals are kept after treatment.

I check each animal before it goes home to make sure it is well.

Nurses look after animals in the recovery area. They feed them and give them medicine.

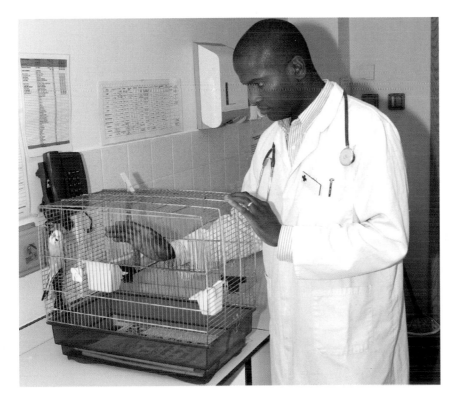

Being a vet is a challenging job because you never know what animal you will be treating.

Finishing work

At the end of my shift, I talk to the vet who is taking over. I tell her about any problems or urgent cases.

I sort out my paperwork in
the office. I check the list of cases
for tomorrow on the computer.
Then it is time to go home.

Vet equipment

A **muzzle** is sometimes put over a dog's mouth to stop it nipping a vet when it is scared.

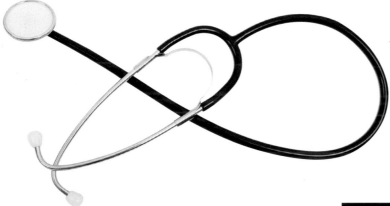

A **stethoscope** is used to listen to the heartbeat.

An **x-ray** is a picture that shows the inside of an animal.

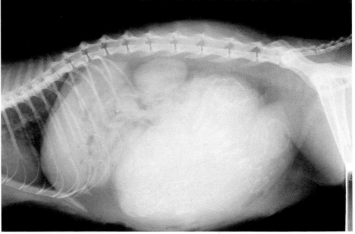

These **metal instruments** are specially cleaned after an operation. Then they are wrapped in a bundle ready for next time.

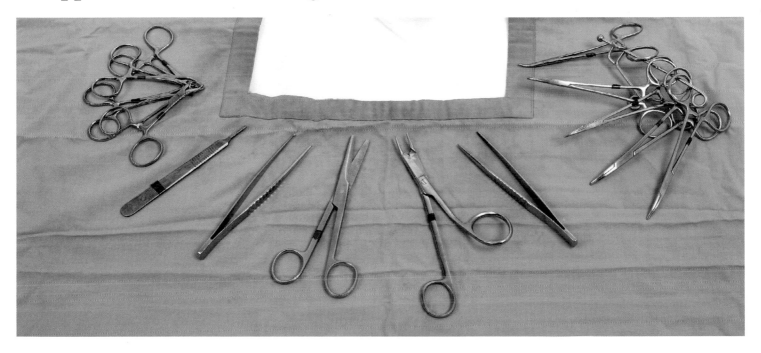

These **clogs** are worn in the operating theatre. If the vets wore their own shoes they might bring in dirt and germs.

Pet information

I CAN GO OUT FOR A WALK

Nigel works at a Blue Cross animal hospital. The Blue Cross is one of the UK's oldest animal charities. It has several animal hospitals in London, and it also has rehoming centres all over the country. A rehoming centre is where they keep dogs, cats and other pets who need new homes.

If you are thinking about getting a pet you can find out about the Blue Cross on their website: www.bluecross.org.uk

**There are lots of questions
to ask before you get a pet:**

- Who will pay for vet care and health checks?
- Do you have enough room to keep a pet?
- Who will feed your pet?
- Are you ready to spend lots of time with a pet?
- Who will look after it when you are on holiday?

You can find information about choosing a pet or
looking after your pet on: www.allaboutpets.org.uk

Glossary and index

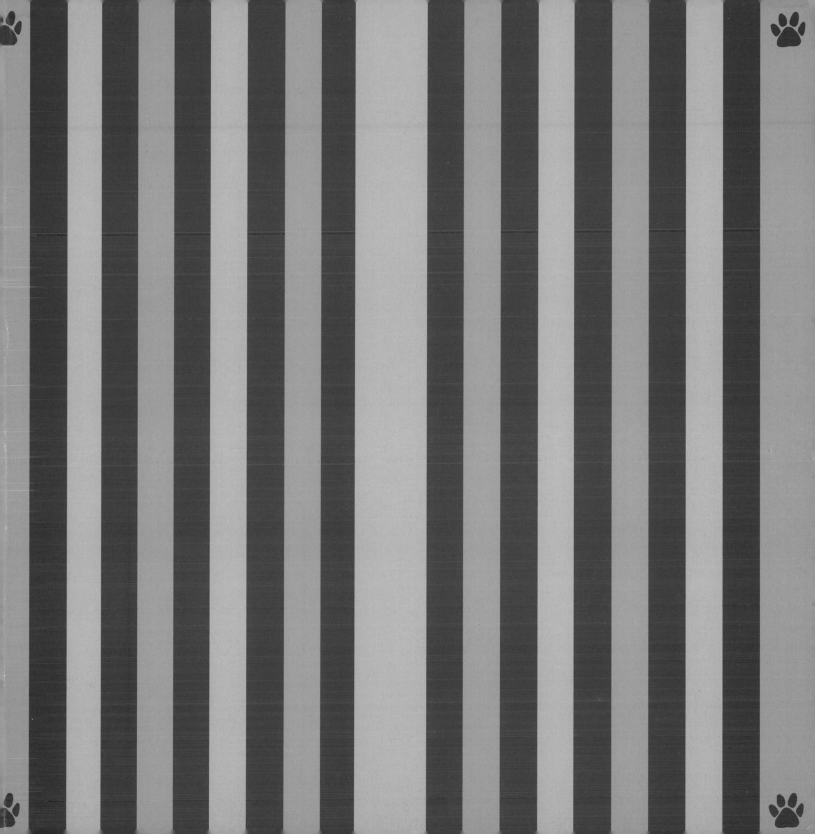

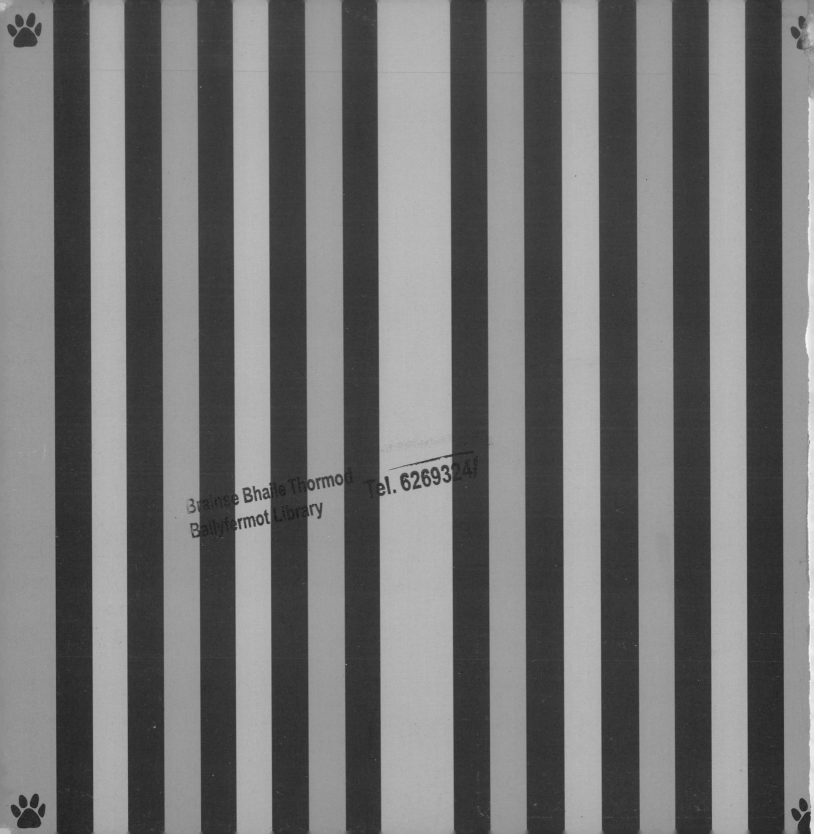